ALAN BENNETT has been one of our leading dramatists since the success of Beyond the Fringe in the 1960s. His television series *Talking Heads* has become a modern-day classic, as have many of his works for the stage, including Forty Years On, A Question of Attribution, The Madness of George III (together with the Oscar-nominated screenplay The Madness of King George), The Lady in the Van (together with the screenplay for the film adaptation, directed by his longtime collaborator Nicholas Hytner and starring Maggie Smith and Alex Jennings) and an adaptation of Kenneth Grahame's The Wind in the Willows. At the National Theatre, London, The History Boys won numerous awards including Evening Standard and Critics' Circle awards for Best Play, an Olivier for Best New Play and the South Bank Award. On Broadway, The History Boys won five New York Drama Desk Awards, four Outer Critics' Circle Awards, a New York Drama Critics' Award, a New York Drama League Award and six Tonys. The Habit of Art opened at the National in 2009; in 2012, People, as well as the two short plays Hymn and Cocktail Sticks, was also staged there. His collection of prose Writing Home was a number one bestseller. Untold Stories won the PEN/Ackerley Prize for autobiography, 2006. Recent works of fiction are The Uncommon Reader and Smut: Two Unseemly Stories.

Also by Alan Bennett

STAGE PLAYS

Plays One: Forty Years On, Getting On,
Habeas Corpus, Enjoy
Plays Two: Kafka's Dick, The Insurance Man,
The Old Country, An Englishman Abroad,
A Question of Attribution
The Lady in the Van
Office Suite
The Madness of George III
The Wind in the Willows
The History Boys
People
The Habit of Art
Cocktail Sticks

TELEVISION PLAYS

Me, I'm Afraid of Virginia Woolf: A Day Out,
Sunset Across the Bay, A Visit from Miss Prothero,
Me, I'm Afraid of Virginia Woolf, Green Forms,
The Old Crowd, Afternoon Off
Rolling Home: One Fine Day, All Day on the Sands,
Our Winnie, Rolling Home, Marks,
Say Something Happened, Intensive Care
Talking Heads 1 and 2

SCREENPLAYS

A Private Function: *The Old Crowd, A Private
Function, Prick Up Your Ears, 102 Boulevard
Haussmann, The Madness of King George,
The Lady in the Van*
The History Boys: *The film*

AUTOBIOGRAPHY

The Lady in the Van
Writing Home
Untold Stories
A Life Like Other People's

FICTION

Four Stories: *The Laying on of Hands, The Clothes
They Stood Up In, Father! Father! Burning Bright,
The Lady in the Van*
The Uncommon Reader

THE LADY
IN THE VAN

ALAN BENNETT

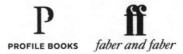

PROFILE BOOKS   *faber and faber*

This edition published in Great Britain in 2015 by
Profile Books Ltd
3 Holford Yard, Bevin Way
London WC1X 9HD
www.profilebooks.com

and

Faber & Faber Limited
74–77 Great Russell Street
London WC1B 3DA

First published in 1989 by *London Review of Books*,
28 Little Russell Street, London WC1A 2HN. *The Lady in the Van*
is included in Alan Bennett's collection of prose, *Writing Home*,
published by Faber & Faber Ltd; also in *Four Stories* published by
Profile Books

Typeset in Quadraat
Designed by Peter Campbell
Printed and bound by CPI Group (UK) Ltd, Croydon, CR0 4YY
Author photo: Anthony Crolla

A CIP catalogue record for this book is available from the
British Library.

ISBN 978 178125 5407

THE LADY IN THE VAN

Good nature, or what is often considered as such, is the most selfish of all virtues: it is nine times out of ten mere indolence of disposition.

William Hazlitt
'On the Knowledge of Character' (1822)

'I ran into a snake this afternoon,' Miss Shepherd said. 'It was coming up Parkway. It was a long, grey snake – a boa constrictor possibly. It looked poisonous. It was keeping close to the wall and seemed to know its way. I've a feeling it may have been heading for the van.' I was relieved that on this occasion she didn't demand that I ring the police, as she regularly did if anything out of the ordinary occurred. Perhaps this was too out of the ordinary (though it turned out the pet shop in Parkway had been broken into the previous night, so she may have seen a snake). She brought her mug over and I made her a drink, which she took back to the van. 'I thought I'd better tell you,' she said, 'just to be on the safe side. I've had some close shaves with snakes.'

This encounter with the putative boa constrictor was in the summer of 1971, when Miss Shepherd and her van had for some months been at a permanent halt opposite my house in Camden Town. I had first come across her a few years previously, stood by her van, stalled as usual, near the convent at the top of the street. The convent (which was to have a subsequent career as the Japanese School) was a gaunt reformatory-like building that housed a dwindling garrison of aged nuns and was notable for a striking crucifix attached to the wall overlooking the traffic lights. There was something about the position of Christ, pressing himself against the grim pebbledash

'... Miss Shepherd and her van had for some months been at a permanent halt opposite my house'.

beneath the barred windows of the convent, that called up visions of the Stalag and the searchlight and which had caused us to dub him 'The Christ of Colditz'. Miss Shepherd, not looking un-crucified herself, was standing by her vehicle in an attitude with which I was to become very familiar, left arm extended with the palm flat against the side of the van indicating ownership, the right arm summoning anyone who was fool enough to take notice of her, on this occasion me. Nearly six foot, she was a commanding figure, and would have been more so had she not been kitted out in greasy raincoat, orange skirt, Ben Hogan golfing-cap and carpet slippers. She would be going on sixty at this time.

She must have prevailed on me to push the van as far as Albany Street, though I recall nothing of the exchange. What I do remember was being overtaken by two policemen in a panda car as I trundled the van across Glouc-ester Bridge; I thought that, as the van was certainly holding up the traffic, they might have lent a hand. They were wiser than I knew. The other feature of this first run-in with Miss Shepherd was her driving technique. Scarcely had I put my shoulder to the back of the van, an old Bedford, than a long arm was stretched elegantly out of the driver's window to indicate in textbook fashion that she (or rather I) was moving off. A few yards further on, as we were about to turn into Albany Street, the arm emerged again, twirling elaborately in the air to indicate that we were branching left, the movement done with such boneless grace that this section of the Highway Code might have been choreographed by Petipa with Ulanova at the wheel. Her 'I am coming to a halt' was less poised, as she had plainly not expected me to give up pushing and shouted angrily back that it was the other end of Albany Street she wanted, a mile further on. But I had had enough by this time and left her there, with no thanks for my trouble. Far from it. She even climbed out of the van and came running after me, shouting that I had no business abandoning her, so that passers-by looked at me as if I had done some injury to this pathetic scarecrow. 'Some people!' I suppose I thought, feeling foolish that I'd been taken for a ride (or taken her for one) and cross that I'd fared worse than if I'd never lifted a finger, these mixed feelings to be the invariable aftermath of any transaction involving Miss Shepherd. One seldom was able to do her a good turn without some thoughts of strangulation.

It must have been a year or so after this, and so some time in the late sixties, that the van first appeared in Gloucester Crescent. In those days the street was still a bit of a mixture. Its large semi-detached villas had originally been built to house the Victorian middle class, then it had gone down in the world, and, though it had never entirely decayed, many of the villas degenerated into rooming-houses and so were among the earliest candidates for what is now called 'gentrification' but which was then called 'knocking through'. Young professional couples, many of them in journalism or television, bought up the houses, converted them and (an invariable feature of such conversions) knocked the basement rooms together to form a large kitchen/dining-room. In the mid-sixties I wrote a BBC TV series, *Life in NW1*, based on one such family, the Stringalongs, whom Mark Boxer then took over to people a cartoon strip in the *Listener*, and who kept cropping up in his drawings for the rest of his life. What made the social set-up funny was the disparity between the style in which the new arrivals found themselves able to live and their progressive opinions: guilt, put simply, which today's gentrifiers are said famously not to feel (or 'not to have a problem about'). We did have a problem, though I'm not sure we were any better for it. There was a gap between our social position and our social obligations. It was in this gap that Miss Shepherd (in her van) was able to live.

October 1969. When she is not in the van Miss S. spends much of her day sitting on the pavement in Parkway, where she has a pitch outside Williams & Glyn's Bank. She sells tracts, entitled 'True View: Mattering Things', which she writes herself, though this isn't something she will admit. 'I sell them, but so far as the authorship is concerned I'll say they are anonymous and that's as far as I'm prepared to go.' She generally chalks the gist of the current pamphlet on the pavement, though with no attempt at artistry. 'St Francis FLUNG money from him' is today's message, and prospective customers have to step over it to get into the bank. She also makes a few coppers selling pencils. 'A gentleman came the other day and said that the pencil he had bought from me was the best pencil on the market at the present time. It lasted him three months. He'll be back for another one shortly.' D., one of the more conventional neighbours (and not a knocker-through), stops me and says, 'Tell me, is she a *genuine* eccentric?'

April 1970. Today we moved the old lady's van. An obstruction order has been put under the windscreen wiper, stating that it was stationed outside number 63 and is a danger to public health. This order, Miss S. insists, is a statutory order: 'And statutory means standing – in this case standing outside number 63 – so, if the van is moved on, the order will be invalid.' Nobody ventures to argue with this, but she can't decide whether her next pitch should be outside number 61 or further on. Eventually she decides there is 'a nice space' outside 62 and plumps for that. My neighbour Nick Tomalin and I heave away at the back of the van, but while she is gracefully indicating that she is moving off (for all of the fifteen feet) the van doesn't budge. 'Have you let the handbrake off?'

Nick Tomalin asks. There is a pause. 'I'm just in the process of taking it off.' As we are poised for the move, another Camden Town eccentric materializes, a tall, elderly figure in long overcoat and Homburg hat, with a distinguished grey moustache and in his buttonhole a flag for the Primrose League. He takes off a grubby canary glove and leans a shaking hand against the rear of the van (OLU246), and when we have moved it forward the few statutory feet he puts on his glove again, saying, 'If you should need me I'm just round the corner' (i.e. in Arlington House, the working men's hostel).

I ask Miss S. how long she has had the van.

'Since 1965,' she says, 'though don't spread that around. I got it to put my things in. I came down from St Albans in it, and plan to go back there eventually. I'm just pedalling water at the moment. I've always been in the transport line. Chiefly delivery and chauffeuring. You know,' she says mysteriously – 'renovated army vehicles. And I've got good topography. I always have had. I knew Kensington in the blackout.'

This van (there were to be three others in the course of the next twenty years) was originally brown, but by the time it had reached the Crescent it had been given a coat of yellow. Miss S. was fond of yellow ('It's the papal colour') and was never content to leave her vehicles long in their original trim. Sooner or later she could be seen moving slowly round her immobile home, thoughtfully touching up the rust from a tiny tin of primrose paint, looking, in her long dress and sunhat, much as Vanessa Bell would have

'This van (there were to be three others in the course of the next twenty years) was originally brown, but … all her vehicles ended up looking as if they had been given a coat of badly made custard or plastered with scrambled egg.'

looked had she gone in for painting Bedford vans. Miss S. never appreciated the difference between car enamel and ordinary gloss paint, and even this she never bothered to mix. The result was that all her vehicles ended up looking as if they had been given a coat of badly made custard or plastered with scrambled egg. Still, there were few occasions on which one saw Miss Shepherd genuinely happy and one of them was when she was putting paint on. A few years before she died she went in for a Reliant Robin (to put more of her things in). It was actually yellow to start with, but that didn't save it from an additional coat, which she applied as Monet might have done, standing back to judge the effect of each brush-stroke. The Reliant stood outside my gate. It was towed away earlier this year, a scatter of yellow drops on the kerb all that remains to mark its final parking place.

January 1971. Charity in Gloucester Crescent takes refined forms. The publishers next door are bringing out some classical volume and to celebrate the event last night held a Roman dinner. This morning the au pair was to be seen knocking at the window of the van with a plate of Roman remains. But Miss S. is never easy to help. After twelve last night I saw her striding up the Crescent waving her stick and telling someone to be off. Then I heard a retreating middle-class voice say plaintively, 'But I only asked if you were all right.'

June 1971. Scarcely a day passes now without some sort of incident involving the old lady. Yesterday evening around ten a sports car swerves over to her side of the road so that the driver, rich, smart and in his twenties, can lean over and bang on the side of the van, presumably to flush out for his grinning girlfriend the old witch who lives there. I shout at him and he sounds his horn and roars off. Miss S. of course wants the police called, but I can't see the point, and indeed around five this morning I wake to find two policemen at much the same game, idly shining their torches in the windows in the hope that she'll wake up and enliven a dull hour of their beat. Tonight a white car reverses dramatically up the street, screeches to a halt beside the van, and a burly young man jumps out and gives the van a terrific shaking. Assuming (hoping, probably) he would have driven off by the time I get outside, I find he's still there, and ask him what the fuck he thinks he's doing. His response is quite mild. 'What's up with you then?' he asks. 'You still on the telly? You nervous? You're trembling all over.' He then calls me a fucking cunt and drives off. After all that, of course, Miss S. isn't in the van at all, so I end up as usual more furious with her than I am with the lout.

These attacks, I'm sure, disturbed my peace of mind more than they did hers. Living in the way she did, every day must have brought such cruelties. Some of the stallholders in the Inverness Street market used to persecute her with medieval relish – and children too, who both inflict and suffer such casual cruelties themselves. One night two drunks systematically smashed all the windows of the van, the flying glass cutting her face. Furious over any small liberty, she was only mildly disturbed by this. 'They may have had too much to drink by mistake,' she said. 'That does occur through not having eaten, possibly. I don't want a case.' She was far more interested in 'a ginger feller I saw in Parkway in company with Mr Khruschev. Has he disappeared recently?'

But to find such sadism and intolerance so close at hand began actively to depress me, and having to be on the alert for every senseless attack made it impossible to work. There came a day when, after a long succession of such incidents, I suggested that she spend at least the nights in a lean-to at the side of my house. Initially reluctant, as with any change, over the next two years she gradually abandoned the van for the hut.

In giving her sanctuary in my garden and landing myself with a tenancy that went on eventually for fifteen years I was never under any illusion that the impulse was purely charitable. And of course it made me furious that I had been driven to such a pass. But I wanted a quiet life as much as, and possibly more than, she did. In the garden she was at least out of harm's way.

October 1973. I have run a lead out to the lean-to and now regularly have to mend Miss S.'s electric fire, which she keeps fusing by

plugging too many appliances into the attach-
ment. I sit on the steps fiddling with the fuse
while she squats on her haunches in the hut.
'Aren't you cold? You could come in here. I
could light a candle and then it would be a bit
warmer. The toad's been in once or twice. He
was in here with a slug. I think he may be in love
with the slug. I tried to turn it out and it got very
disturbed. I thought he was going to go for me.'
She complains that there is not enough room
in the shed and suggests I get her a tent, which
she could then use to store some of her things.
'It would only be three feet high and by rights
ought to be erected in a meadow. Then there are
these shatterproof greenhouses. Or something
could be done with old raincoats possibly.'

March 1974. The council are introducing
parking restrictions in the Crescent. Residents'
bays have been provided and yellow lines

drawn up the rest of the street. To begin with, the workmen are very understanding, painting the yellow line as far as the van, then beginning again on the other side so that technically it is still legally parked. However, a higher official has now stepped in and served a removal order on it, so all this week there has been a great deal of activity as Miss S. transports cargoes of plastic bags across the road, through the garden and into the hut. While professing faith in divine protection for the van, she is prudently clearing out her belongings against its possible removal. A notice she has written declaring the council's action illegal twirls idly under the windscreen wiper.

'The notice was served on a Sunday. I believe you can serve search warrants on a Sunday but nothing else, possibly. I should have the Freedom of the Land for the good articles I've sold on the economy.' She is particularly concerned about the tyres of the van which 'may be miraculous. They've only been pumped up twice since 1964. If I get another vehicle'– and Lady W. is threatening to buy her one – 'I'd like them transferred.'

The old van was towed away in April 1974 and another one provided by Lady W. ('a titled Catholic lady', as Miss S. always referred to her). Happy to run to a new (albeit old) van, Lady W. was understandably not anxious to have it parked outside her front door and eventually, and perhaps by now inevitably, the van and Miss S. ended up in my garden. This van was roadworthy, and Miss S. insisted on being the one to drive it through the gate into the garden, a manoeuvre which once again enabled her to go through her full repertoire of hand signals. Once the van was on site Miss S. applied the handbrake with such determination that, like Excalibur, it could never thereafter be released, rusting so firmly into place that when the van came to be moved ten years later it had to be hoisted over the wall by the council crane.

This van (and its successor, bought in 1983) now occupied a paved area between my front door and the garden gate, the bonnet of the van hard by my front step, its rear door, which Miss S. always used to get in and out of, a few feet from the gate. Callers at the house had to squeeze past the back of the van and come down the side, and while they waited for my door to be opened they would be scrutinized from behind the murky windscreen by Miss Shepherd. If they were unlucky, they would find the rear door open with Miss S. dangling her large white legs over the back. The interior of the van, a midden of old clothes, plastic bags and half-eaten food, was not easy to ignore, but should anyone Miss S. did not know venture to speak to her she would promptly tuck her legs back and wordlessly shut the door. For the first few years of her sojourn in the garden I would try and explain to mystified callers how this situation had arisen, but after a while I ceased to care, and when I didn't mention it nor did anyone else.

At night the impression was haunting. I had run a cable out from the house to give her light and heating, and through the ragged draperies that hung over the windows of the van a visitor would glimpse Miss S.'s spectral figure, often bent over in prayer or lying on her side like an effigy on a tomb, her face resting on one hand, listening to Radio 4. Did she hear any movements she would straightaway switch off the light and wait, like an animal that has been disturbed, until she was sure the coast was clear and could put the light on again. She retired early and would complain if anyone called or left late at night. On one occasion Coral Browne was coming away from the house with her husband, Vincent Price, and they were talking quietly. 'Pipe down,' snapped the voice from the van, 'I'm trying to sleep.' For someone who had brought terror to millions it was an unexpected taste of his own medicine.

December 1974. Miss S. has been explaining to me why the old Bedford (the van not the music-hall) ceased to go, 'possibly'. She had put in some of her home-made petrol, based on a recipe for petrol substitute she read about several years ago in a newspaper. 'It was a spoonful of petrol, a gallon of water and a pinch of something you could get in every High Street. Well, I got it into my head, I don't know why, that it was bicarbonate of soda, only I think I was mistaken. It must be either sodium chloride or sodium nitrate, only I've since been told sodium chloride is salt and the man in Boots wouldn't sell me the other, saying it might cause explosions. Though I think me being an older person he knew I would be more responsible. Though not all old ladies perhaps.'

February 1975. Miss S. rings, and when I open the door she makes a bee-line for the kitchen stairs. 'I'd like to see you. I've called several times. I wonder whether I can use the toilet first.' I say I think this is pushing it a bit. 'I'm not pushing it at all. I just will do the interview better if I can use the toilet first.' Afterwards she sits down in her green mac and purple headscarf, the knuckles of one large mottled hand resting on the clean, scrubbed table and explains how she has devised a method of 'getting on the wireless'. I was to ask the BBC to give me a phone-in programme ('something someone like you could get put on in a jiffy') and then she would ring me up from the house. 'Either that or I could get on *Petticoat Line*. I know a darn sight more on moral matters than most of them. I could sing my song over the telephone. It's a lovely song, called "The End of the World"' (which is pure *Beyond the Fringe*). 'I won't commit myself to singing it – not at this moment – but I probably would. Some sense should be said and knowledge known. It could all be anonymous. I could be called The Lady Behind the Curtain. Or A Woman of Britain. You could take a *nom-de-plume* view of it.' This idea of The Woman Behind the Curtain has obviously taken her fancy and she begins to expand on it, demonstrating where the curtain could be, her side of it coincidentally taking in the television and the easy chair. She could be behind the curtain, she explains, do her periodic broadcasts, and the rest of the time 'be a guest at the television and take in some civilization. Perhaps there would be gaps filled with nice classical music. I know one: Prelude and "Liebestraum" by Liszt. I believe he was a Catholic priest. It means "love's dream", only not the sexy stuff. It's the love of God and the sanctification of labour and so on, which would recommend it to celibates like you and me, possibly.' Shocked at this tentative bracketing of our conditions, I quickly get rid of her and, though it's a bitter cold night, open the windows wide to get rid of the smell.

The Woman Behind the Curtain remained a favourite project of hers, and in 1976 she wrote to Aiman (sic) Andrews: 'Now that This is Your Life is ended, having cost too much etc., I might be able to do a bit as The Lady Behind the Curtain. All you need do is put a curtain up to hide me but permit words of sense to come forth in answer to some questions. Sense is needed.' Hygiene was needed too, but possibly in an effort to persuade me about being behind the curtain she brought the subject up herself. 'I'm by nature a very clean person. I have a testimonial for a Clean Room, awarded me some years ago, and my aunt, herself spotless, said I was the cleanest of my mother's children, particularly in the unseen places.' I never fathomed her toilet arrangements. She only once asked me to buy her toilet rolls ('I use them to wipe my face'), but whatever happened in that department I took to be part of some complicated arrangement involving the plastic bags she used to hurl from the van every morning. When she could still manage stairs she did very occasionally use my loo, but I didn't encourage it; it was here, on the threshold of the toilet, that my charity stopped short. Once when I was having some building work done (and was, I suppose, conscious of what the workmen were thinking), I very boldly said there was a smell of urine. 'Well, what can you expect when they're raining bricks down on me all day? And then I think there's a mouse. So that would make a cheesy smell, possibly.'

Miss S.'s daily emergence from the van was

highly dramatic. Suddenly and without warning the rear door would be flung open to reveal the tattered draperies that masked the terrible interior. There was a pause, then through the veils would be hurled several bulging plastic sacks. Another pause, before slowly and with great caution one sturdy slippered leg came feeling for the floor before the other followed and one had the first sight of the day's wardrobe. Hats were always a feature: a black railwayman's hat with a long neb worn slightly on the skew so that she looked like a drunken signalman or a French guardsman of the 1880s; there was her Charlie Brown pitcher's hat; and in June 1977 an octagonal straw table-mat, tied on with a chiffon scarf and a bit of cardboard for the peak. She also went in for green eyeshades. Her skirts had a telescopic appearance, as they had often been lengthened many times over by the simple expedient of sewing a strip of extra cloth around the hem, though with no attempt at matching. One skirt was made by sewing several orange dusters together. When she fell foul of authority she put it down to her clothes. Once, late at night, the police rang me from Tunbridge Wells. They had picked her up on the station, thinking her dress was a nightie. She was indignant. 'Does it look like a nightie? You see lots of people wearing dresses like this. I don't think this style can have got to Tunbridge Wells yet.'

Miss S. seldom wore stockings, and alternated between black pumps and brown carpet slippers. Her hands and feet were large, and she was what my grandmother would have called 'a big-boned woman'. She was middle class and spoke in a middle-class way, though her querulous and often resentful demeanour tended to obscure this; it wasn't a gentle or a genteel voice. Running through her vocabulary was a streak of schoolgirl slang. She wouldn't say she was tired, she was 'all done up'; petrol was 'juice'; and if she wasn't keen on doing something she'd say 'I'm darned if I will.' All her conversation was impregnated with the vocabulary of her peculiar brand of Catholic fanaticism ('the dire importance of justice deeds'). It was the language of the leaflets she wrote, the 'possibly' with which she ended so many of her sentences an echo of the 'Subject to the Roman Catholic Church in her rights etc.' with which she headed every leaflet.

May 1976. I have had some manure delivered for the garden and, since the manure heap is not far from the van, Miss S. is concerned that people passing might think the smell is coming from there. She wants me to put a notice on the gate to the effect that the smell is the manure, not her. I say no, without adding, as I could, that the manure actually smells much nicer.

I am working in the garden when Miss B., the

social worker, comes with a boxful of clothes.

Miss S. is reluctant to open the van door, as she is listening to *Any Answers*, but eventually she slides on her bottom to the door of the van and examines the clothes. She is unimpressed.

MISS S.: I only asked for one coat.

MISS B.: Well, I brought three just in case you wanted a change.

MISS S.: I haven't got room for three. Besides, I was planning to wash this coat in the near future. That makes four.

MISS B.: This is my old nursing mac.

MISS S.: I have a mac. Besides, green doesn't suit me. Have you got the stick?

MISS B.: No. That's being sent down. It had to be made specially.

MISS S.: Will it be long enough?

MISS B.: Yes. It's a special stick.

MISS S.: I don't want a special stick. I want an ordinary stick. Only longer. Does it have a rubber thing on it?

When Miss B. has gone, Miss S. sits at the door of the van slowly turning over the contents of the box like a chimpanzee, sniffing them and holding them up and muttering to herself.

June 1976. I am sitting on the steps mending my bike when Miss S. emerges for her evening stroll. 'I went to Devon on Saturday,' she said. 'On this frisbee.' I suppose she means freebie, a countrywide concession to pensioners that BR ran last weekend. 'Dawlish I went to. People very nice. The man over the loudspeaker called us Ladies and Gentlemen, and so he should. There was one person shouted, only he wasn't one of us – the son of somebody, I think.' And almost for the first time ever she smiled, and said how they had all been bunched up trying to get into this one carriage, a great crowd, and how she had been hoisted up. 'It would have made a film,' she said. 'I thought of you.'

And she stands there in her grimy raincoat, strands of lank grey hair escaping from under her headscarf. I am thankful people had been nice to her, and wonder what the carriage must have been like all that hot afternoon. She then tells me about a programme on Francis Thompson she'd heard on the wireless, how he had tried to become a priest but had felt he had failed in his vocation, and had become a tramp. Then, unusually, she told me a little of her own life, and how she tried to become a nun on two occasions, had undergone instruction as a novice, but was forced to give it up on account of ill-health, and that she had felt for many years that she had failed. But that this was wrong, and it was not a failure. 'If I could have had more modern clothes, longer sleep and better air, possibly, I would have made it.'

'A bit of a spree,' she called her trip to Dawlish. 'My spree.'

June 1977. On this the day of the Jubilee, Miss S. has stuck a paper Union Jack in the cracked back-window of the van. It is the only one in the Crescent. Yesterday she was wearing a headscarf and pinned across the front of it a blue Spontex sponge fastened at each side with a large safety pin, the sponge meant to form some kind of peak against the (very watery) sun. It looked like a favour worn by a medieval knight, or a fillet to ward off evil spirits. Still, it was better than last week's effort, an Afrika Korps cap from Lawrence Corner: Miss Shepherd – Desert Fox.

September 1979. Miss S. shows me a photograph she has taken of herself in a cubicle at Waterloo. She is very low in the frame, her mouth pulled down, the photo looking as if it has been taken after death. She is very pleased with it. 'I don't take a good photograph usually. That's the only photograph I've seen looks anything like me.'

She wants two copies making of it. I say that it would be easier for her to go back to Waterloo and do two more. No – that would 'take it out of her'. 'I had one taken in France once when I was twenty-one or twenty-two. Had to go into the next village for it. I came out cross-eyed. I saw someone else's photo on their bus-pass and she'd come out looking like a nigger. You don't want to come out like a nigger if you can help it, do you?'

June 1980. Miss S. has gone into her summer rig: a raincoat turned inside out, with brown canvas panels and a large label declaring it the Emerald Weatherproof. This is topped off with a lavender chiffon scarf tied round a sun visor made from an old cornflakes packet. She asks me to do her some shopping. 'I want a small packet of Eno's, some milk and some jelly babies. The jelly babies aren't urgent. Oh and,

Mr Bennett, could you get me one of those little bottles of whisky? I believe Bell's is very good. I don't drink it – I just use it to rub on.'

August 1980. I am filming, and Miss S. sees me leaving early each morning and returning late. Tonight her scrawny hand comes out with a letter marked 'Please consider carefully':

An easier way for Mr Bennett to earn could be possibly with my cooperative part. Two young men could follow me in a car, one with a camera to get a funny film like 'Old Mother Riley Joins Up' possibly. If the car stalls they could then push it. Or they could go on the buses with her at a distance. Comedy happens without trying sometimes, or at least an interesting film covering a Senior Citizen's use of the buses can occur. One day to Hounslow, another to Reading or Heathrow. The bus people ought to be pleased, but it might need their permission. Then Mr Bennett could put his feet up more and rake it in, possibly.

October 1980. Miss S. has started hankering after a caravan trailer and has just missed one she saw in *Exchange and Mart*: 'little net curtains all round, three bunks'. 'I wouldn't use them all, except', she says ominously, 'to put things on. Nice little windows – £275. They said it was sold, only they may have thought I was just an old tramp … I was thinking of offering to help Mrs Thatcher with the economy. I wouldn't ask any money, as I'm on social security, so it would come cheap for her. I might ask her for some perks, though. Like a caravan. I would write to her but she's away. I know what's required. It's perfectly simple: Justice.'

No political party quite catered to Miss S.'s views, though the National Front came close. She was passionately anti-Communist, and as long ago as 1945 had written a letter to Jesus 'concerning the dreadful situation feared from the Yalta agreement'. The trouble was that her political opinions, while never moderate, were always tempered by her idiosyncratic view of the human physiognomy. Older was invariably wiser, which is fair if debatable, except that with Miss S. taller was wiser too. But height had its drawbacks, and it was perhaps because she was tall herself that she believed a person's height added to their burdens, put them under some strain. Hence, though she was in sympathy with Mr Heath on everything except the Common Market, 'I do think that Mr Wilson, person-ally, may have seen better in regard to Europe, being on the Opposition bench with less salary and being older, smaller and under less strain.' She was vehemently opposed to the Common Market – the 'common' always underlined when she wrote about it on the pavement, as if it were the sheer vulgarity of the economic union she particularly objected to. Never very lucid in her leaflets, she got especially confused over the EEC. 'Not long ago a soul wrote, or else was considering writing (she cannot recall as to which and it may have been something of either) that she disassociated from the Common Market entry and the injustices feared concerning it, or something like that.' 'Enoch', as she invariably called Mr Powell, had got it right, and she wrote him several letters telling him so, but in the absence of a wholly congenial party she founded her own, the Fidelis Party. 'It will be a party caring for Justice (and as such not needing opposition). Justice in the world today with its gigantic ignorant conduct requires the rule of a Good Dictator, possibly.'

Miss S. never regarded herself as being at the bottom of the social heap. That place was occupied by 'the desperate poor' – i.e. those with no roof over their heads. She herself was 'a cut above those in dire need', and one of her responsibilities in society she saw as interceding for them and for those whose plight she thought Mrs Thatcher had overlooked. Could it be brought to her attention (and she wrote Mrs T. several letters on the subject), alleviation would surely follow.

Occasionally she would write letters to other public figures. In August 1978 it was to the College of Cardinals, then busy electing a Pope. 'Your Eminences. I would like to suggest humbly that an older Pope might be admirable. Height can count towards knowledge too probably.' However this older (and hopefully taller) Pope she was recommending might find the ceremony a bit of a trial, so, ever the expert on headgear, she suggests that 'at the Coronation there could be a not so heavy crown, of light plastic possibly or cardboard for instance.'

February 1981. Miss S. has flu, so I am doing her shopping. I wait every morning by the side window of the van and, with the dark interior and her grimy hand holding back the tattered purple curtain, it is as if I am at the confessional. The chief items this morning are ginger nuts ('very warming') and grape juice. 'I think this is what they must have been drinking at Cana,' she says as I hand her the bottle. 'Jesus wouldn't have wanted them rolling about drunk, and this is non-alcoholic. It wouldn't do for everyone, but in my opinion it's better than champagne.'

October 1981. The curtain is drawn aside this morning and Miss S., still in what I take to be her nightclothes, talks of 'the discernment of spirits' that enabled her to sense an angelic presence near her when she was ill. At an earlier period, when she had her pitch outside the bank, she had sensed a similar angelic presence, and now, having seen his campaign leaflet, who should this turn out to be, 'possibly', but Our Conservative Candidate Mr Pasley-Tyler. She embarks on a long disquisition on her well-worn theme of age in politics. Mrs Thatcher is too young and travels too much. Not like President Reagan. 'You wouldn't catch him making all those U-turns round Australia.'

January 1982. 'Do you see he's been found, that American soldier?' This is Colonel Dozo, kidnapped by the Red Brigade and found after a shoot-out in a flat in Padua. 'Yes, he's been found,' she says triumphantly, 'and I know who found him.' Thinking it unlikely she has an acquaintance in the Italian version of the SAS, I ask whom she means. 'St Anthony of course. The patron saint of lost things. St Anthony of Padua.' 'Well,' I want to say, 'he didn't have far to look.'

May 1982. As I am leaving for Yorkshire, Miss S.'s hand comes out like the Ancient Mariner's:

do I know if there are any steps at Leeds Station? 'Why?' I ask warily, thinking she may be having thoughts of camping on my other doorstep. It turns out she just wants somewhere to go for a ride, so I suggest Bristol. 'Yes, I've been to Bristol. On the way back I came through Bath. That looked nice. Some beautifully parked cars.' She then recalls driving her reconditioned army vehicles and taking them up to Derbyshire. 'I did it in the war,' she says. 'Actually I overdid it in the war,' and somehow that is the thin end of the wedge that has landed her up here, yearning for travel on this May morning forty years later.

'Land' is a word Miss S. prefers to 'country'. 'This land ...' Used in this sense, it's part of the rhetoric if not of madness at any rate of obsession. Jehovah's Witnesses talk of 'this land', and the National Front. Land is country plus destiny – country in the sight of God. Mrs Thatcher talks of 'this land'.

February 1983. A. telephones me in Yorkshire to say that the basement is under three inches of water, the boiler having burst. When told that the basement has been flooded, Miss S.'s only comment is 'What a waste of water.'

April 1983. 'I've been having bad nights,' says Miss S., 'but if I were elected I might have better nights.' She wants me to get her nomination papers so that she can stand for Parliament in the coming election. She would be the Fidelis Party candidate. The party, never very numerous, is now considerably reduced. Once she could count on five votes but now there are only two, one of whom is me, and I don't like to tell her I'm in the SDP. Still, I promise to write to the town hall for nomination papers. 'There's no kitty as yet,' she says, 'and I wouldn't want to do any of the meeting people. I'd be no good at that. The secretaries can do that (you

get expenses). But I'd be very good at voting –
better than they are, probably.'

May 1983. Miss S. asks me to witness her
signature on the nomination form. 'I'm
signing,' she says: 'are you witnessing?' She has
approached various nuns to be her nominees.
'One sister I know would have signed but I
haven't seen her for some years and she's got
rather confused in the interim. I don't know
what I'll do about leaflets. It would have to be
an economy job – I couldn't run to the expense.
Maybe I'll just write my manifesto on the
pavement; that goes round like wildfire.'

May 1983. Miss S. has received her nomination
papers. 'What should I describe myself as?' she
asks through the window slit. 'I thought Elderly
Spinster, possibly. It also says Title. Well my
title is' – and she laughs one of her rare laughs

– 'Mrs Shepherd. That's what some people call me out of politeness. And I don't deny it. Mother Teresa always says she's married to God. I could say I was married to the Good Shepherd, and that's what it's to do with, Parliament, looking after the flock. When I'm elected, do you think I shall have to live in Downing Street or could I run things from the van?'

I speak to her later in the day and the nomination business is beginning to get her down. 'Do you know anything about the Act of 1974? It refers to disqualifications under it. Anyway, it's all giving me a headache. I think there may be another election soon after this one, so it'll have been good preparation anyway.'

June 1984. Miss S. has been looking in *Exchange and Mart* again and has answered an advert for a white Morris Minor. 'It's the kind of car I'm used to – or I used to be used to. I feel the need to be mobile.' I raise the matter of a licence and insurance, which she always treats as tiresome formalities. 'What you don't understand is that I am insured. I am insured in heaven.' She claims that since she had been insured in heaven there has not been a scratch on the van. I point out that this is less to do with the celestial insurance than with the fact that the van is parked the whole time in my garden. She concedes that when she was on the road the van did used to get the occasional knock. 'Somebody came up behind me once and scratched the van. I wanted him to pay something – half-a-crown I think it was. He wouldn't.'

October 1984. Some new staircarpet fitted today. Spotting the old carpet being thrown out, Miss S. says it would be just the thing to put on the roof of the van to deaden the sound of rain. This exchange comes just as I am leaving for work, but I say that I do not want the van festooned with bits of old carpet – it looks bad enough as it is. When I come back in the evening I find half the carpet remnants slung over the roof. I ask Miss S. who has put them there, as she can't have done it herself. 'A friend,' she says mysteriously. 'A well-wisher.' Enraged, I pull down a token piece but the majority of it stays put.

April 1985. Miss S. has written to Mrs Thatcher applying for a post in 'the Ministry of Transport advisory, to do with drink and driving and that'. She also shows me the text of a letter she is proposing to send to the Argentinian Embassy on behalf of General Galtieri. 'What he doesn't understand is that Mrs Thatcher isn't the Iron Lady. It's me.'

To Someone in Charge of Argentina. 19 April 1985

Dear Sir,

I am writing to help mercy towards the poor general who led your forces in the war actually as a person of true knowledge more than might be. I was concerned with Justice, Love and, in a manner of speaking, I was in the war, as it were, shaking hands with your then leader, welcoming him in spirit (it may have been to do with love of Catholic education for Malvinas for instance) greatly meaning kindly negotiators etc. ... but I fear that he may have thought it was Mrs Thatcher welcoming him in that way and it may hence have unduly influenced him.

Therefore I beg you to have mercy on him indeed. Let him go, reinstate him, if feasible. You may read publicly this letter if you wish to explain mercy etc.

I remain.

Yours truly

A Member of the Fidelis Party

(Servants of Justice)

P.S. *Others may have contributed to undue influence also.*
P.P.S. *Possibly without realizing it.*
Translate into Argentinian if you shd wish.

Sometime in 1980 Miss S. acquired a car, but before she'd managed to have more than a jaunt or two in it ('It's a real goer!') it was stolen and later found stripped and abandoned in the basement of the council flats in Maiden Lane. I went to collect what was left ('though the police may require it for evidence, possibly') and found that even in the short time she'd had the Mini she'd managed to stuff it with the usual quota of plastic bags, kitchen rolls and old blankets, all plentifully doused in talcum powder. When she got a Reliant Robin in 1984 it was much the same, a second wardrobe as much as a second car. Miss Shepherd could afford to splash out on these vehicles because being parked in the garden meant that she had a permanent address, and so qualified for full social security and its various allowances. Since her only outgoings were on food, she was able to put by something and had an account in the Halifax and quite a few savings certificates. Indeed I heard people passing say, 'You know she's a millionaire,' the inference being no one in their right mind would let her live there if she weren't.

Her Reliant saw more action than the Mini, and she would tootle off in it on a Sunday morning, park on Primrose Hill ('The air is better'), and even got as far as Hounslow. More often than not, though, she was happy (and I think she was happy then) just to sit in the Reliant and rev the engine. However, since she generally chose to do this first thing on Sunday morning, it didn't endear her to the neighbours. Besides, what she described as 'a lifetime with motors' had failed to teach her was that revving a car does not charge the battery, so that when it regularly ran down I had to take it out and recharge it, knowing full well this would just mean more revving. ('No,' she insisted, 'I may be going to Cornwall next week, possibly.') This recharging of the battery wasn't really the issue: I was just ashamed to be seen delving under the bonnet of such a joke car.

March 1987. The nuns up the road – or, as Miss S. always refers to them, 'the sisters' – have taken to doing some of her shopping. One of them leaves a bag on the back step of the van this morning. There are the inevitable ginger nuts, and several packets of sanitary towels. I can see these would be difficult articles for her to ask me to get, though to ask a nun to get them would seem quite hard for her too. They form some part of her elaborate toilet arrangements, and are occasionally to be seen laid drying across the soup-encrusted electric ring.

As the postman says this morning, 'The smell sometimes knocks you back a bit.'

May 1987. Miss S. wants to spread a blanket over the roof (in addition to the bit of carpet) in order to deaden the sound of the rain. I point out that within a few weeks it will be dank and disgusting. 'No,' she says – 'weather-beaten.'

She has put a Conservative poster in the side window of the van. The only person who can see it is me.

This morning she was sitting at the open door of the van and as I edge by she chucks out an empty packet of Ariel. The blanket hanging over the pushchair is covered in washing powder. 'Have you spilt it?' I inquire. 'No,' she says crossly, irritated at having to explain the obvious. 'That's washing powder. When it rains, the blanket will get washed.' As I work at my table now I can see her bending over the pushchair, picking at bits of soap flakes and redistributing them over the blanket. No rain is at the moment forecast.

June 1987. Miss S. has persuaded the social services to allocate her a wheelchair, though what she's really set her heart on is the electric version.

MISS S.: That boy over the road has one. Why not me?

ME: He can't walk.

MISS S: How does he know? He hasn't tried.

ME: Miss Shepherd, he has spina bifida.

MISS S: Well, I was round-shouldered as a child. That may not be serious now, but it was quite serious then. I've gone through two wars, an infant in the first and not on full rations, in the ambulances in the second, besides being failed by the ATS. Why should old people be disregarded?

Thwarted in her ambition for a powered chair, Miss S. compensated by acquiring (I never found out where from) a second wheelchair ('in case the other conks out, possibly'). The full inventory of her wheeled vehicles now read: one van; one Reliant Robin; two wheelchairs; one folding pushchair; one folding (two-seater) pushchair. Now and again I would thin out the pushchairs by smuggling one on to a skip. She would put down this disappearance to children (never a favourite), and the number would shortly be made up by yet another wheelie from Reg's junk stall. Miss S. never mastered the technique of self-propulsion in the wheelchair because she refused to use the inner handwheel ('I can't be doing with all that silliness'). Instead, she preferred to punt herself along with two walking sticks, looking in the process rather like a skier on the flat. Eventually I had to remove the handwheel ('The extra weight affects my health').

'Miss S. never mastered the technique of self-propulsion
in the wheelchair ... instead, she preferred to punt herself
along with two walking sticks, looking in the process
rather like a skier on the flat.'

July 1987. Miss S. (bright-green visor, purple skirt, brown cardigan, turquoise fluorescent ankle socks) punts her way out through the gate in the wheelchair in a complicated manoeuvre which would be much simplified did she just push the chair out, as well she can. A passer-by takes pity on her, and she is whisked down to the market. Except not quite whisked, because the journey is made more difficult than need be by Miss S.'s refusal to take her feet off the ground, so the Good Samaritan finds himself pushing a wheelchair continually slurred and braked by these large, trailing, carpet-slippered feet. Her legs are so thin now the feet are as slack and flat as those of a camel.

Still, there will be one moment to relish on this, as on all these journeys. When she had been pushed back from the market, she will tell (and it is tell: there is never any thanks) whoever is pushing the chair to leave her opposite the gate but on the crown of the road. Then, when she thinks no one is looking, she lifts her feet, pushes herself off, and freewheels the few yards down to the gate. The look on her face is one of pure pleasure.

October 1987. I have been filming abroad. 'When you were in Yugoslavia,' asks Miss S., 'did you come across the Virgin Mary?' 'No,' I say, 'I don't think so.' 'Oh, well, she's appearing there. She's been appearing there every day for several years.' It's as if I've missed the major tourist attraction.

January 1988. I ask Miss S. if it was her birthday yesterday. She agrees guardedly. 'So you're seventy-seven.' 'Yes. How did you know?' 'I saw it once when you filled out the census form.' I give her a bottle of whisky, explaining that it's just to rub on. 'Oh. Thank you.' Pause.

'Mr Bennett. Don't tell anybody.' 'About the whisky?' 'No. About my birthday.' Pause. 'Mr Bennett.' 'Yes?' 'About the whisky either.'

March 1988. 'I've been doing a bit of spring cleaning,' says Miss S., kneeling in front of a Kienholzlike tableau of filth and decay. She says she has been discussing the possibility of a bungalow with the social worker, to which she would be prepared to contribute 'a few hundred or so'. It's possible that the bungalow might be made of asbestos, 'but I could wear a mask. I wouldn't mind that, and of course it would be much better from the fire point of view.' Hands in mittens made from old socks, a sanitary towel drying over the ring, and a glossy leaflet from the Halifax offering 'fabulous investment opportunities'.

April 1988. Miss S. asks me to get Tom M. to take a photograph of her for her new bus-pass. 'That would make a comedy, you know – sitting on a bus and your bus-pass out of date. You could make a fortune out of that with very little work involved, possibly. I was a born tragedian,' she says, 'or a comedian possibly. One or the other anyway. But I didn't realize it at the time. Big feet.' She pushes out her red, unstockinged ankles. 'Big hands.' The fingers stained brown. 'Tall. People trip over me. That's comedy. I wish they didn't, of course. I'd like it easier, but there it is. I'm not suggesting you do it,' she says hastily, feeling perhaps she's come too near self-revelation, 'only it might make people laugh.' All of this is said with a straight face and no hint of a smile, sitting in the wheelchair with her hands pressed between her knees and her baseball cap on.

May 1988. Miss S. sits in her wheelchair in the road, paintpot in hand, dabbing at the bodywork of the Reliant, which she will shortly enter, start, and rev for a contented half-hour before switching off and paddling down the road in her wheelchair. She has been nattering at Tom M. to mend the clutch, but there are conditions. It mustn't be on Sunday, which is the feast of St Peter and St Paul and a day of obligation. Nor can it be the following Sunday apparently, through the Feast of the Assumption falling on the Monday and being transferred back to the previous day. Amid all the chaos of her life and now, I think, more or less incontinent, she trips with fanatical precision through this liturgical minefield.

September 1988. Miss S. has started thinking about a flat again, though not the one the council offered her a few years ago. This time she has her eye on something much closer to home. My home. We had been talking outside, and I left her sitting on the step in the hall while I came back to work. This is often what happens: me sitting at my table, wanting to get on, Miss S. sitting outside rambling. This time she goes on talking about the flat, soliloquizing almost, but knowing that I can hear. 'It need only be a little flat, even a room possibly. Of course, I can't manage stairs, so it would have to be on the ground floor. Though I'd pay to have a lift put in.' (Louder.) 'And the lift wouldn't be wasted. They'd have it for their old age. And they'll have to be thinking about their old age quite soon.' The tone of it is somehow familiar from years ago. Then I realize it's like one of the meant-to-be-overheard soliloquies of Richmal Cromp-ton's William.

Her outfit this morning: orange skirt, made out of three or four large dusters; a striped blue satin jacket; a green headscarf – blue eyeshield topped off by a khaki peaked cap with a skull-and-crossbones badge and Rambo across the peak.

February 1989. Miss S.'s religion is an odd mixture of traditional faith and a belief in the power of positive thinking. This morning, as ever, the Reliant battery is running low and she asks me to fix it. The usual argument takes place:

ME: Well, of course it's run down. It will run down unless you run the car. Revving up doesn't charge it. The wheels have to go round.

MISS S.: Stop talking like that. This car is not the same. There are miracles. There is faith. Negative thoughts don't help. (*She presses the starter again and it coughs weakly.*) There, you see. The devil's heard you. You shouldn't say negative things.

The interior of the van now indescribable.

March 1989. Miss S. sits in the wheelchair trying to open the sneck of the gate with her walking-stick. She tries it with one end, then reverses the stick and tries with the other. Sitting at my table, trying to work, I watch her idly, much as one would watch an ant trying to get round some obstacle. Now she bangs on the gate to attract the attention of a passer-by. Now she is wailing. Banging and wailing. I go out. She stops wailing, and explains she has her washing to do. As I manoeuvre her through the gate, I ask her if she's fit to go. Yes, only she will need help. I explain that I can't push her there. (Why can't I?) No, she doesn't want that. Would I just push her as far as the corner? I do so. Would I just push her a bit further? I explain that I can't take her to the launderette. (And anyway there is no launderette any more, so which launderette is she going to?) Eventually, feeling like Fletcher Christian (only not Christian) abandoning Captain Bligh, I leave her in the wheelchair outside Mary H.'s. Someone will come along. I would be more ashamed if I did not feel, even when she is poorly, that she knows exactly what she's about.

March 1989. There is a thin layer of talcum powder around the back door of the van and odd bits of screwed up tissues smeared with what may or may not be shit, though there is no doubt about the main item of litter, which is a stained incontinence pad. My method of retrieving these items would not be unfamiliar at Sellafield. I don rubber gloves, put each hand inside a plastic bag as an additional protection, then, having swept the faecal artefacts together, gingerly pick them up and put them in the bin. 'Those aren't all my rubbish,' comes a voice from the van. 'Some of them blow in under the gate.'

April 1989. Miss S. has asked me to telephone the social services, and I tell her that a social worker will be calling. 'What time?' 'I don't know. But you're not going to be out. You haven't been out for a week.' 'I might be. Miracles do happen. Besides, she may not be able to talk to me. I may not be at the door end of the van. I might be at the other end.' 'So she can talk to you there.' 'And what if I'm in the middle?'

Miss C. thinks her heart is failing. She calls her Mary. I find this strange, though it is of course her name.

April 1989. A staple of Miss S.'s shopping-list these days is sherbet lemons. I have a stock of them in the house, but she insists I invest in yet more so that a perpetual supply of sherbet lemons may never be in doubt. 'I'm on them now. I don't want to have to go off them.'

I ask her if she would like a cup of coffee.

'Well, I wouldn't want you to go to all that trouble. I'll just have half a cup.'

Towards the end of her life Miss S. was befriended by an ex-nurse who lived locally. She put me in touch with a day centre who agreed to take Miss Shepherd in, give her a bath and a medical examination and even a bed in a single room where she could stay if she wanted. In retrospect I see I should have done something on the same lines years before, except that it was only when age and illness had weakened Miss Shepherd that she would accept such help. Even then it was not easy.

27 April 1989. A red ambulance calls to take Miss S. to the day centre. Miss B. talks to her for a while in the van, gradually coaxing her out and into the wheelchair, shit streaks over her swollen feet, a piece of toilet roll clinging

to one scaly ankle. 'And if I don't like it,' she keeps asking, 'can I come back?' I reassure her, but, looking at the inside of the van and trying to cope with the stench, I find it hard to see how she can go on living here much longer. Once she sees the room they are offering her, the bath, the clean sheets, I can't imagine her wanting to come back. And indeed she makes more fuss than usual about locking the van door, which suggests she accepts that she may not be returning. I note how, with none of my distaste, the ambulance driver bends over her as he puts her on the hoist, his careful rearrangement of her greasy clothing, pulling her skirt down over her knees in the interests of modesty. The chair goes on the hoist, and slowly she rises and comes into view above the level of the garden wall and is wheeled into the ambulance. There is a certain distinction about her as she leaves, a Dorothy Hodgkin of vagabonds, a derelict Nobel Prize-winner, the heavy folds of her grimy face set in a kind of resigned satisfaction. She may even be enjoying herself.

When she has gone I walk round the van noting the occasions of our battle: the carpet tiles she managed to smuggle on to the roof, the blanket strapped on to muffle the sound of the rain, the black bags under the van stuffed with her old clothes – sites of skirmishes all of which I'd lost. Now I imagine her bathed and bandaged and cleanly clothed and starting a new life. I even see myself visiting and taking flowers.

This fantasy rapidly fades when around 2.30 Miss S. reappears, washed and in clean clothes, it's true, and with a long pair of white hospital socks over her shrunken legs, but obviously very pleased to be back. She has a telephone number where her new friends can be contacted, and she gives it to me. 'They can be reached', she says, 'any time – even over the holiday. They're on a long-distance bleep.'

As I am leaving for the theatre, she bangs on the door of the van with her stick. I open the door. She is lying wrapped in clean white sheets on a quilt laid over all the accumulated filth and rubbish of the van. She is still worrying that I will have her taken to hospital. I tell her there's no question of it and that she can stay as long as she wants. I close the door, but there is another bang and I reassure her again. Once more I close the door, but she bangs again.' Mr Bennett.' I have to strain to hear. 'I'm sorry the van's in such a state. I haven't been able to do any spring cleaning.'

28 April. I am working at my table when I see Miss B. arrive with a pile of clean clothes for Miss Shepherd, which must have been washed for her at the day centre yesterday. Miss B. knocks at the door of the van, then opens it,

looks inside and – something nobody has ever done before – gets in. It's only a moment before she comes out, and I know what has happened before she rings the bell. We go back to the van where Miss Shepherd is dead, lying on her left side, flesh cold, face gaunt, the neck stretched out as if for the block, and a bee buzzing round her body.

It is a beautiful day, with the garden glittering in the sunshine, strong shadows by the nettles, and bluebells out under the wall, and I remember how in her occasional moments of contemplation she would sit in the wheelchair and gaze at the garden. I am filled with remorse for my harsh conduct towards her, though I know at the same time that it was not harsh. But still I never quite believed or chose to believe she was as ill as she was, and I regret too all the questions I never asked her. Not that she would have answered them. I have a strong impulse to stand at the gate and tell anyone who passes.

Miss B. meanwhile goes off and returns with a nice doctor from St Pancras who seems scarcely out of her teens. She gets into the van, takes the pulse in Miss S.'s outstretched neck, checks her with a stethoscope and, to save an autopsy, certifies death as from heart failure. Then comes the priest to bless her before she is taken to the funeral parlour, and he, too, gets into the van – the third person to do so this morning, and all of them without distaste or ado in what to me seem three small acts of heroism. Stooping over the body, his bright white hair brushing the top of the van, the priest murmurs an inaudible prayer and makes a cross on Miss S.'s hands and head. Then they all go off and I come inside to wait for the undertakers.

I have been sitting at my table for ten minutes before I realize that the undertakers have been here all the time, and that death nowadays comes (or goes) in a grey Ford transit van that is standing outside the gate. There are three undertakers, two young and burly, the third older and more experienced – a sergeant, as it were, and two corporals. They bring out a rough grey-painted coffin, like a prop a conjuror might use, and, making no comment on the surely extraordinary circumstances in which they find it, put a sheet of white plastic bin-liner over the body and manhandle it into their magic box, where it falls with a bit of a thud. Across the road, office workers stroll down from the Piano Factory for their lunch, but nobody stops or even looks much, and the Asian woman who has to wait while the box is carried over the pavement and put in the (other) van doesn't give it a backward glance.

Later I go round to the undertakers to arrange the funeral, and the manager apologizes for their response when I had originally phoned. A woman had answered, saying, 'What exactly is it you want?' Not thinking callers rang undertakers with a great variety of requests, I was nonplussed. Then she said briskly, 'Do you want someone taking away?' The undertaker explains that her seemingly unhelpful manner was because she thought my call wasn't genuine. 'We get so many hoaxes these days. I've often gone round to collect a corpse only to have it open the door.'

9 *May.* Miss Shepherd's funeral is at Our Lady of Hal, the Catholic church round the corner. The service has been slotted into the ten o'clock mass, so that, in addition to a contingent of neighbours, the congregation includes what I take to be regulars: the fat little man in thick glasses and trainers who hobbles along to the church every day from Arlington House; several nuns, among them the ninety-nine-year-old sister who was in charge when Miss S. was briefly a novice; a woman in a green straw hat like an upturned plant pot who eats toffees

throughout; and another lady who plays the harmonium in tan slacks and a tea-cosy wig. The server, a middle-aged man with white hair, doesn't wear a surplice, just ordinary clothes with an open-necked shirt, and, but for knowing all the sacred drill, might have been roped in from the group on the corner outside The Good Mixer. The priest is a young Irish boy with a big, red peasant face and sandy hair, and he, too, stripped of his cream-coloured cassock, could be wielding a pneumatic drill in the roadworks outside. I keep thinking about these characters during the terrible service, and it reinforces what I have always known: that I could never be a Catholic because I'm such a snob, and that the biggest sacrifice Newman made when he turned his back on the C of E was the social one.

Yet kindness abounds. In front of us is a thin old man who knows the service backwards, and seeing we have no prayer books he lays down

his own on top of his copy of the Sun, goes
back up the aisle to fetch us some, and hands
them round, all the time saying the responses
without faltering. The first hymn is Newman's
'Lead Kindly Light', which I try and sing, while
making no attempt at the second hymn, which
is 'Kum Ba Ya'. The priest turns out to have a
good strong voice, though its tone is more
suited to 'Kum Ba Ya' than to Newman and J. B.
Dykes. The service itself is wet and wandering,
even more so than the current Anglican equiva-
lent, though occasionally one catches in the
watered-down language a distant echo of 1662.
Now, though, arrives the bit I dread, the cele-
bration of fellowship, which always reminds
me of the warm-up Ned Sherrin insisted on
inflicting on the studio audience before Not
So Much a Programme, when everyone had to
shake hands with their neighbour. But again
the nice man who fetched us the prayer books
shames me when he turns round without any

fuss or embarrassment and smilingly shakes my hand. Then it is the mass proper, the priest distributing the wafers to the ninety-nine-year-old nun and the lady with the plant pot on her head, as Miss S. lies in her coffin at his elbow. Finally there is another hymn, this one by the (to me) unknown hymnodist Kevin Norton, who's obviously reworked it from his unsuccessful entry for the Eurovision Song Contest; and with the young priest acting as lead singer, and the congregation a rather subdued backing group, Miss Shepherd is carried out.

The neighbours, who are not quite mourners, wait on the pavement outside as the coffin is hoisted on to the hearse. 'A cut above her previous vehicle,' remarks Colin H.; and comedy persists when the car accompanying the hearse to the cemetery refuses to start. It's a familiar scene, and one which I've played many times, with Miss S. waiting inside her vehicle as wellwishers lift the bonnet, fetch leads and give it a jump start. Except this time she's dead.

Only A. and I and Clare, the ex-nurse who lately befriended Miss S., accompany the body, swept around Hampstead Heath at a less than funereal pace, down Bishop's Avenue and up to the St Pancras Cemetery, green and lush this warm, sunny day. We drive beyond the scattered woods to the furthest edge where stand long lines of new gravestones, mostly in black polished granite. Appropriately, in view of her lifelong love of the car, Miss S. is being buried within sight and sound of the North Circular Road, one carriageway the other side of the hedge, with juggernauts drowning the words of the priest as he commits the body to the earth. He gives us each a go with his little plastic bottle of holy water, we throw some soil into the grave, and then everybody leaves me to whatever solitary thoughts I might have, which are not many, before we are driven back to Camden Town – life reasserted when the under-taker drops us handily outside Sainsbury's.

In the interval between Miss Shepherd's death and her funeral ten days later I found out more about her life than I had in twenty years. She had indeed driven ambulances during the war, and was either blown up or narrowly escaped death when a bomb exploded nearby. I'm not sure that her eccentricity can be put down to this any more than to the legend, mentioned by one of the nuns, that it was the death of her fiancé in this incident that 'tipped her over'. It would be comforting to think that it is love, or the death of it, that imbalances the mind, but I think her early attempts to become a nun and her repeated failures ('too argumentative,' one of the sisters said) point to a personality that must already have been quite awkward when she was a girl. After the war she spent some time in mental hospitals, but regularly absconded, finally remaining at large long enough to establish her competence to live unsupervised.

The turning-point in her life came when,

through no fault of hers, a motorcyclist crashed into the side of her van. If her other vans were any guide, this one too would only have been insured in heaven, so it's not surprising she left the scene of the accident ('skedaddled', she would have said) without giving her name or address. The motorcyclist subsequently died, so that, while blameless in the accident, by leaving the scene of it she had committed a criminal offence. The police mounted a search for her. Having already changed her first name when she became a novice, now under very different circumstances she changed her second and, calling herself Shepherd, made her way back to Camden Town and the vicinity of the convent where she had taken her vows. And though in the years to come she had little to do with the nuns, or they with her, she was never to stray far from the convent for the rest of her life.

All this I learned in those last few days. It was as if she had been a character in Dickens whose history has to be revealed and her secrets told in the general setting-to-rights before the happy-ever-after, though all that this amounted to was that at long last I could bring my car into the garden to stand now where the van stood all those years.

POSTSCRIPT (1994)

This account of Miss Shepherd condenses
some of the many entries to do with her that are
scattered through my diaries. Unemphasized
in the text (though deducible from the dates
of the entries) is the formality of her last days.
The Sunday before she died she attended mass,
which she had not done for many months; on
the Wednesday morning she allowed herself to
be taken to be bathed and given clean clothes
and then put to bed in the van on clean sheets;
and that same night she died. The progression
seemed so neat that I felt, when I first wrote
it up, that to emphasize it would cast doubt
on the truth of my account, or at least make it
seem sentimental or melodramatic. However,
the doctor who pronounced Miss Shepherd
dead said that she had known other deaths in
similar circumstances; that it was not (as I had
facetiously wondered) the bath that had killed

her but that to allow herself to be washed and put into clean clothes was both a preparation and an acknowledgement that death was in the offing.

Nor is it plain from the original account how in the period after her death I got to know the facts of her life that she had so long concealed. A few months before, a bout of flu must have made her think about putting her affairs in order and she had shown me an envelope that I might need 'in case anything happens to me, possibly'. I would find the envelope in the place under the banquette where she kept her savings books and other papers. What the envelope contained she did not say, and, when in due course she got over the flu and struggled on, nothing more was said about it.

It was about this time, though, that I had the first and only hint that her name might not be her own. She had, I knew, some money in the Abbey National, and periodically their bright brochures would come through my door – young and happy home-owners pictured gaily striding across their first threshold and entering upon a life of mortgaged bliss.

'Some post, Miss Shepherd,' I would knock on the window and wait for the scrawny hand to come out (nails long and grey; fingers ochre-stained as if she had been handling clay). The brochure would be drawn back into the dim and fetid interior, where it would be a while before it was opened, the packet turned over and over in her dubious hands, the Society's latest exciting offer waiting until she was sure it was not from the IRA. 'Another bomb, possibly. They've heard my views.'

In 1988 the Abbey National were preparing to turn themselves from a building society into a bank, a proposal to which Miss Shepherd for some reason (novelty, possibly) was very much opposed. Before filling in her ballot form, she asked me (and she was careful to couch the question impersonally) if a vote would be valid had the purchaser of the shares changed their name. I said, fairly obviously, that if the shares had been bought in one name then it would be in order to vote in that name. 'Why?' I asked. But I should have known better, and, as so often, having given a teasing hint of some revelation, she refused to follow it up, just shook her head mutely, and snapped shut the window. Except (and this was standard procedure too) as I was passing the van next day her hand came out.

'Mr Bennett. What I said about change of name, don't mention it to anybody. It was just in theory, possibly.'

For some days after Miss Shepherd's death I left the van as it was, not from piety or anything to do with decorum but because I couldn't face getting into it, and though I put on a new padlock I made no attempt to extract her bank books or locate the necessary envelope. But the news had got round, and when one afternoon I came home to find a scrap dealer nosing about I realized I had to grit my teeth (or hold my nose) and go through Miss Shepherd's possessions.

To do the job properly would have required a team of archaeologists. Every surface was covered in layers of old clothes, frocks, blankets and accumulated papers, some of them undisturbed for years and all lying under a crust of ancient talcum powder. Sprinkled impartially over wet slippers, used incontinence pads and half-eaten tins of baked beans, it was of a virulence that supplemented rather than obliterated the distinctive odour of the van. The narrow aisle between the two banks of seats where Miss Shepherd had knelt, prayed and slept was trodden six inches deep in sodden debris, on which lay a top dressing of old food, Mr Kipling cakes, wrinkled apples, rotten oranges and everywhere batteries – batteries loose, batteries in packets, batteries that had split and oozed black gum on to the prehistoric sponge cakes and ubiquitous sherbet lemons that they lay among. A handkerchief round my face, I lifted one of the banquettes where in the hollow beneath she had told me her bank books were hidden. The underside of the seat was alive with moths and maggots, but the books were there, together with other documents she considered valuable: an MOT certificate for her Reliant, long expired; a receipt for some repairs to it done three years before; an offer of a fortnight of sun and sea in the Seychelles that came with some car wax. What there was not was the envelope. So there was nothing for it but to excavate the van, to go through the festering debris in the hope of finding the note she had promised to leave, and with it perhaps her history.

Searching the van, I was not just looking for the envelope; sifting the accumulated refuse of fifteen years, I was hoping for some clue as to what it was that had happened to make Miss

Shepherd want to live like this. Except that I kept coming across items that suggested that living 'like this' wasn't all that different from the way people ordinarily lived. There was a set of matching kitchen utensils, for instance – a ladle, a spatula, a masher for potatoes – all of them unused. They were the kind of thing my mother bought and hung up in the kitchen, just for show, while she went on using the battered old-faithfuls kept in the knife drawer. There were boxes of cheap soap and, of course, talcum powder, the cellophane wrapping unbreached; they too had counterparts in the dressing-table drawer at home.

Another item my mother hoarded was toilet rolls, and here were a dozen. There was a condiment set, still in its box. When, amid such chaos, can she have hoped to use that particular appurtenance of gentility? But when did we ever use ours, stuck permanently in the sideboard cupboard in readiness for the social life my parents never had or ever really wanted? The more I laboured, the less peculiar the van seemed – its proprieties and aspirations no different from those with which I had been brought up.

There was cash here too. In a bag Miss Shepherd carried round her neck there had been nearly £500, and peeling off the soggy layers from the van floor I collected about £100 more. Taking into account the money in various building societies and her National Savings certificates, Miss Shepherd had managed to save some £6,000. Since she was not entitled to a pension, most of this must have been gleaned from the meagre allowance she got from the DHSS. I am not sure whether under the present regime she would have been praised for her thrift or singled out as a sponger. Arch-Tory though she was, she seems a prime candidate for Mr Lilley's little list, a paid-up member of the Something for Nothing society. I would just like to have seen him tell her so.

Modest though Miss Shepherd's estate was, it was more than I'd been expecting and made the finding of the envelope more urgent. So I went through the old clothes again, this time feeling gingerly in the pockets and shaking out the greasy blankets in a blizzard of moth and 'French Fern'. But there was nothing, only her bus-pass, the grim photograph looking as if it were taken during the siege of Stalingrad and hardly auguring well for the comedy series she had once suggested I write on the subject. I was about to give up, having decided that she must have kept the envelope on her and that it had been taken away with the body, when I came upon it, stiff with old soup and tucked into the glove compartment along with another cache of batteries and sherbet lemons, and marked 'Mr Bennett, if necessary'.

Still looking for some explanation ('I am like this, possibly, because ...'), I opened the envelope. True to form, even in this her final communication Miss Shepherd wasn't prepared to give away any more than she had to. There was just a man's name, which was not her own, and a phone number in Sussex.

I finished cleaning out the van, scraped down the aisle, and opened all the windows and doors so that for the first time since she had moved in it was almost sweet-smelling – only not, because sweet in an awful way was how she had made it smell. My neighbour, the artist David Gentleman, who ten years before had done a lightning sketch of Miss Shepherd watching the removal of an earlier van, now came and did a romantic drawing of this her last vehicle, the grass growing high around it and the tattered curtains blowing in the spring breeze.

2 *May* 1989. This afternoon comes a rather
dapper salvage man who, fifteen years ago,
refused to execute a council order for the
removal of one of Miss Shepherd's earlier vans
on the grounds that someone was living in it.
So he says anyway, though it's perhaps just
to establish his claim. He stands there on the
doorstep, maybe waiting to see if I am going
to mention a price; I wait too, wondering if he
is going to mention a charge. Silence on both
sides seems to indicate that the transaction is
over with no payment on either side, and within
the hour he is back with his lift-ing-gear. Tom
M. takes photographs as the van is hauled like
an elephant's carcass through the gate and up
the ramp, the miraculous tyres still happily
inflated; the salvage man scrawls 'On Tow' in
the thick dirt on the windscreen; stood by the
bonnet I pose for a final photograph (which
doesn't come out); and the van goes off for
the last time up the Crescent, leaving the drive

feeling as wide and empty as the Piazza San Marco.

5 *May* 1989. 'Mr Bennett?' The voice is a touch military and quite sharp, though with no accent to speak of and nothing to indicate this a man who must be over eighty. 'You've sent me a letter about a Miss Shepherd, who seems to have died in your drive. I have to tell you I have no knowledge of such a person.' A bit nonplussed, I describe Miss Shepherd and her circumstances and give her date of birth. There is a slight pause.

'Yes. Well it's obviously my sister.'

He tells me her history and how, returning from Africa just after the war, he found her persecuting their mother, telling her how wicked she was and what she should and shouldn't eat, the upshot being that he finally had his sister committed to a mental hospital in Hayward's Heath. He gives her subsequent history, or as much of it as he knows, saying that the last time he had seen her was three years ago. He's direct and straightforward and doesn't disguise the fact that he feels guilty – about having her committed yet cannot see how he could have done otherwise, how they never got on, and how he cannot see how I have managed to put up with her all these years. I tell him about the money, slightly expecting him to change his tune and stress how close they had really been. But not a bit of it. Since they hadn't got on he wants none of it, saying I should have it. When I disclaim it too, he tells me to give it to charity.

Anna Haycraft (Alice Thomas Ellis) had mentioned Miss S.'s death in her *Spectator* column, and I tell him about this, really to show that his sister did have a place in people's affections and wasn't simply a cantankerous old woman. 'Cantankerous is not the word,' he says, and laughs. I sense a wife there, and after I put the phone down I imagine them mulling over the call.

I mull it over too, wondering at the bold life she has had and how it contrasts with my own timid way of going on – living, as Camus said, slightly the opposite of expressing. And I see how the location of Miss Shepherd and the van in front but to the side of where I write is the location of most of the stuff I write about; that too is to the side and never what faces me.

Over a year later, finding myself near the village in Sussex where Mr F. lived, I telephoned and asked if I could call. In the meantime I'd written about Miss Shepherd in the *London Review of Books* and broadcast a series of talks about her on Radio 4.

17 June 1990. Mr and Mrs F. live in a little bungalow in a modern estate just off the main road. I suppose it was because of the unhesitating fashion in which he'd turned down her legacy that I was expecting something grander; in fact Mrs F. is disabled and their circumstances are obviously quite modest, which makes his refusal more creditable than I'd thought. From his phone manner I'd been expecting someone brisk and businesslike, but he's a plumpish, jolly man, and both he and his wife are full of laughs. They give me some lovely cake, which he's baked (Mrs F. being crippled with arthritis) and then patiently answer my questions.

The most interesting revelation is that as a girl Miss S. was a talented pianist and had studied in Paris under Cortot, who had told her she should have a concert career. Her decision to become a nun put an end to the piano, 'and that can't have helped her state of mind' says Mr F.

He recalls her occasional visits, when she would never come in by the front door but lope across the field at the back of the house and climb over the fence. She never took any notice of Mrs F., suspecting, rightly, that women were likely to be less tolerant of her than men.

He says all the fiancé stuff, which came via the nuns, is nonsense; she had no interest in men, and never had. When she was in the ambulance service she used to be ribbed by the other drivers, who asked her once why she had never married. She drew herself up and said, 'Because I've never found the man who could satisfy me.' Mystified by their laughter she went home and told her mother, who laughed too.

Mr F. has made no secret of the situation to his friends, particularly since the broadcasts, and keeps telling people he's spent his life trying to make his mark and here she is, having lived like a tramp, more famous than he'll ever be. But he talks about his career in Africa, how he still works as a part-time vet, and I come away thinking what an admirable pair they are, funny and kind and as good in practice as she was in theory – the brother Martha to his sister's Mary.

Sometimes now hearing a van door I think, 'There's Miss Shepherd,' instinctively looking up to see what outfit she's wearing this morning. But the oil patch that marked the site of the van has long since gone, and the flecks of yellow paint on the pavement have all but faded. She has left a more permanent legacy, though, and not only to me. Like diphtheria and Brylcreem, I associate moths with the forties, and until Miss Shepherd took up residence in the drive I thought them firmly confined to the past. But just as it was clothes in which the plague was reputedly spread to the Derbyshire village of Eyam so it was a bundle of Miss Shepherd's clothes, for all they were firmly done up in a black plastic bag, that brought the plague to my house, spreading from the bag to the wardrobe and from the wardrobe to the carpets, the appearance of a moth the signal for frantic clapping and savage stamping. On her death my vigorous cleaning of the van broadcast the plague more widely, so that now many of my neighbours have come to share in this unwanted legacy.

Her grave in the Islington St Pancras Cemetery is scarcely less commodious than the narrow space she slept in the previous twenty years. It is unmarked, but I think as someone so reluctant to admit her name or divulge any information about herself, she would not have been displeased by that.

ALAN BENNETT

Untold Stories

'Not only my book
of the year, it is my
book of the decade.'
Nigel Slater, *Observer*

Alan Bennett

Smut

two unseemly stories

Alan
Bennett

The Uncommon Reader

'A masterpiece of comic brevity.'
Observer

Six Poets
Hardy to Larkin

An Anthology by Alan
Bennett

'Classic Bennett, full of wisdom and wit.'
Simon Armitage